Soul Search

The Answers You Need to
the Biggest Questions You're Asking

BRANDON THOMAS

Soul Search: The Answers You Need to the Biggest Questions You're Asking

Published 2016

ISBN: 978-1-942464-30-3

Printed in the United States of America

To order additional copies, write to:
Passionate Life Ministries
8237 Mid Cities Blvd.
North Richland Hills, TX 76182

CONTENTS

Let's Get Started

Civilizations throughout history have invented countless false religions as a way of connecting with some kind of higher power. And today, tens of thousands of these belief systems are still practiced all over the world.

But no matter how foreign or far-fetched a religious system may seem, they all search for answers to the Four Big Cosmic Questions that are at the core of our existence…

Where did we come from?

Why are we here?

How did it all go wrong?

Where are we going?

The purpose of this book isn't just to show you how the Bible answers these questions, but to lead you on a journey, *a soul search*, that takes you straight to the heart of a God who longs to satisfy your desire to know yourself truly… and to know Him deeply.

Maybe today you find yourself at a crossroads in life.

Perhaps you're facing a big financial decision and don't know what to do. Maybe you feel a change in your career coming up, but you're paralyzed with fear about how it could impact your life. Or it could be that you've been struggling in your marriage, and you're wondering if it's really worth it to try to make it work.

Every question like these that we seek to answer in life… no matter how difficult or perplexing they may seem… can be answered once you answer the Four Big Cosmic Questions that are at the core of our existence.

When we understand the *whys* of our lives, the *whats* will follow.

We can't dodge the questions God has put on our hearts. And though they seem like big mountains far out on the horizon, God has given us the tools we need to climb them and find the answers our souls truly long for.

The religions of the world may seek to help us climb those mountains, but they will always fall short because they're missing the central ingredient that the Bible contains: A loving God who pursues you and me, redeems us from our sins, and invites us to spend eternity with Him.

In the pages that follow, we're going to head straight for those mountains because the answers we seek will take us directly to the heart of God—and His dreams for our lives.

If you're ready, let's jump in!

QUESTION 1
Where Did You Come From?

Every great story has a beginning.

I'm a sci-fi fan, and I've noticed a trend among these kinds of movies in recent years, where they try to explain the origins of human beings. One movie I saw, *Prometheus*, suggests that aliens could have "seeded" our planet with DNA. And eventually, life came crawling out!

There's a reason so many try to tell this story (no matter how ridiculous it seems). It's because they're tapping into a burning desire that exists within every person to know where they came from.

Of course, tapping into this desire is great for making money. Maybe you've seen the commercials for the online services that offer to test your DNA and tell you about your family origins. All you have to do is swab your cheek and—*BOOM!* Instant origins.

We even explore origins in our conversations with others. One of the funniest

things I heard said when we first had a newborn baby was, "She looks so much like her mother."

All I could think was, *No, my wife is WAY better looking than that!*

It's not that we're wrong—it's that we want to understand where we came from. Our origins form the foundation of our story. They give us a framework for interpreting our present and directing our future.

So let's embark on our journey by exploring our foundations—our beginnings recorded in the first book of the Bible…

> *In the beginning God created the heavens and the earth. The earth was formless and empty, and darkness covered the deep waters. And the Spirit of God was hovering over the surface of the waters. Then God said, "Let there be light," and there was light. And God saw that the light was good. Then he separated the light from the darkness. God called the light "day" and the darkness "night." And evening passed and morning came, marking the first day.* (Genesis 1:1-5 NLT)

Here it is… the beginning of it all. God's story begins with "God created"—a process that took six days. And at the end of each day, God

looked back on what He'd made and declared, "It is good."

Then we humans came on the scene in verse 26…

> *Then God said, "Let us make human beings in our image, to be like us. They will reign over the fish in the sea, the birds in the sky, the livestock, all the wild animals on the earth, and the small animals that scurry along the ground."* (Genesis 1:26 NLT)

Now, I have to take a time-out here for a massive footnote.

When God said, "Let us," that's plural. And here we have a very heavy truth: the Trinity. It's the idea that God exists in three persons—Father, Son, and Holy Spirit—but is one in His essence or His being.

You see, before we even came on the scene, God had a perfect relationship with Himself. He didn't create us because He was lonely—as if we could be the friends God never had. He created us for a much deeper reason, which we see in verses 27-28…

> *So God created human beings in his own image. In the image of God he created them; male and female he created them.*

Then God blessed them and said, "Be fruitful and multiply. Fill the earth and govern it. Reign over the fish in the sea, the birds in the sky, and all the animals that scurry along the ground."

Being created in God's image means we are made to fill the earth and rule over it as God's representatives. That's our created purpose.

You're Not an Accident

Now, there's another narrative out there today that attempts to compete with this one. This story tells us that everything we touch, feel, and experience is an accident. It's all a result of matter crashing into itself and arranging itself in such a way that our world and everything in it came into being.

But while you can describe the world without God, it's impossible to describe the world *apart* from God.

One classic illustration of this, which many have used, is discovering a watch in the middle of a forest. You pick it up, and what's the thought that goes through your head? Maybe it's, *Lucky me!*

But any reasonable person would no doubt conclude that someone had dropped it there. Nobody would rationally think, *My goodness...*

look what the trees have done!

You are far more complex than the most expensive watch. There are thousands of miles of veins running through your body. There's no engine created by man that can compete with the engine of the human heart. And when we look subatomically at how we're put together on a molecular level, it's astonishing!

You are a constant reminder that there is a Designer who created you. You were not an accident!

Why You Matter to God

If God created you, then that means He cares for you. God isn't apathetic toward the things He creates. He delights in His creation. As I mentioned, He took a look at everything He'd made and said, "It is good."

When I was 16 years old and first started driving, my parents didn't buy me a car. Instead, they let me use the family car—a Ford Taurus. And man, I was set. At the time, I thought it was the greatest car in the world.

One day my dad told me, "All right, Brandon, I want you to go out there and wash and wax the car." So I went out and did just what he'd asked me to do. I scrubbed as hard as I could to remove every bit of dirt. Then I went

to work waxing, buffing, and rubbing until my arms wouldn't work anymore. It was exhausting.

But when I was done, I looked back at that car and thought, *Wow! That looks incredible!* To me, that 1986 Ford Taurus might as well have been a brand-new Corvette!

There's just something about a job well done. When you use your hands to work on something, there's a real connection with the results. And if I saw that Ford Taurus as a piece of immaculate work, then just imagine how much more God loves and values you, me, and the rest of His creation as the fruit of His labor.

A False Conflict Between the Physical and Spiritual

Now, this action of declaring creation "good" has a number of important implications— one of the main ones is that it breaks down the idea that the physical and spiritual worlds exist in opposition to one another.

In Genesis 1, God, a spiritual being, blesses the physical world. He says, "I made this, and I made it good." That means there's no inherent conflict between the physical and spiritual.

So we can love things that are created. We don't have to feel guilty for enjoying what God has made and blessed. In fact, you're doing

exactly what you were created to do when you enjoy God's gifts in His way.

Did you get that? *Creation is made to be enjoyed God's way.*

There's a reason I want to be sure you understand this. For a good part of history, many have regarded the spiritual world as eternal and good, and the physical world as temporary and evil.

That's why Gandhi gets so much applause for restraining himself from enjoying the physical world. There's something in our minds that says you're more spiritual when you push away physical delights. But God isn't telling us this.

God's creation is good. So you don't have to feel guilty when you eat that big steak dinner. And there's no shame in enjoying the nice car you saved up to buy. Enjoy the physical world God's way. It's His gift to you!

Living Spiritually in a Physical World

I visited Thailand on a mission trip a number of years ago. I was there with a team helping missionaries in the region, and we went to a resort town that was a big draw for tourists from Europe and the United States. This area was popular for a number of reasons—many of them absolutely horrifying.

One of the missionaries took us down the main street of the town, and I saw things I'd never want my kids to see. Utter disregard for humanity. Subjugation of women. Teenage girls (and younger) being sold to men in their 50s and 60s. To call it sickening doesn't do it justice. I asked myself, *How can this be? How can this culture accept this kind of abuse?*

Still grieved over what I had witnessed, I later found myself in a conversation with one of the employees at the hotel where we were staying. I decided to ask this local woman how these kinds of injustices could exist in their town. Her answer was very revealing. In a culture of poverty with mouths to feed and rampant oppression, she basically said, "We are here on this earth to make other people happy. So we tell ourselves, 'Make others happy... it will all be over soon.'"

What she said revealed a deadly misunderstanding of the physical world, which led to the heartbreaking abuse of her people. This belief—that what happens in the physical life, even to one's own body, is of little to no value compared to eternity—misrepresents the heart of the One who created the physical world we live in. God created us to bring Him glory—starting now! This means we can appreciate the beauty of His creation, savor the pleasures in life, and seek to bring about justice on earth. Our Creator has a design for how to live this life we have been

given, so we seek to learn and follow His design.

When you believe the physical world is bad and the spiritual world is the ultimate good, the results can be dangerous and even devastating. Behaviors and choices can be deemed irrelevant because "it doesn't really matter." Even Christ-followers can subconsciously decide to just scrape by in this life until heaven comes, doing little to right the wrongs and bring relief to those in great need. Oppression and abuse become "just the way it is." They are viewed as things to be endured—even, as I saw in Thailand, accepted.

This is not the good news Jesus gives us! The Bible says, "Learn to do good. Seek justice. Help the oppressed. Defend the cause of orphans. Fight for the rights of widows" (Isaiah 1:17 NLT). Those aren't things we'll do in heaven. We're commanded to do them now!

Our God says physical life is good. It's worth something. And we all share a calling to seek justice, because it will give a glimpse of God's Kingdom to those who are far from it. That doesn't mean we'll right all of the wrongs today—but it means we should never be content to say, "That's just the way it is."

A Lesson from Hobbits

If you've ever read the books in The Lord of the Rings trilogy by J. R. R. Tolkien or seen

the movies, then you're familiar with the little fictitious creatures called Hobbits.

Now, you might know that Tolkien was a close friend of C. S. Lewis, author of The Chronicles of Narnia series, as well as many other books. Both men were Christians (Tolkien was a Catholic, and Lewis was an Anglican), and both infused profound spiritual truth into their fictitious writings.

Tolkien's Hobbits were an interesting band of little people. Known for their love of life, they ate, they drank, and they danced merrily. It was a way of life for them.

This behavior earned Hobbits the reputation in Middle Earth (the name of Tolkien's Lord of the Rings universe) for being happy-go-lucky, not having a care in the world. So it was thought that if they ever encountered hardship, they'd run for the hills.

But that wasn't true in the least. In his prologue to *The Fellowship of the Ring*, Tolkien writes of Hobbits…

> *Nonetheless, ease and peace had left this people still curiously tough. They were, if it came to it, difficult to daunt or to kill; and they were, perhaps, so unwearyingly fond of good things not least because they could, when put to it, do without*

them, and could survive rough handling by grief, foe, or weather in a way that astonished those who did not know them well and looked no further than their bellies and their well-fed faces.

In other words, when others saw how well Hobbits could suffer, they were shocked.

Throughout The Lord of the Rings series, it's clear that Tolkien intends the Hobbit characters to represent followers of Christ. As Scripture says, "It is good for people to eat, drink, and enjoy their work under the sun during the short life God has given them…" (Ecclesiastes 5:18 NLT).

We can throw parties, enjoy good food, and have fun without feeling guilty. But when those good things are taken away, we can still have life because our eyes are focused *beyond* this world.

You were created by God. You bear His image. He welcomes you into relationship with Him. And He showers us with His goodness, His grace, and His gifts. We are then like reflectors, pointing all of that goodness, grace, and those gifts back to Him.

Identity: The Ultimate Source of Your Joy

What does that mean for us? It means you and I aren't limited to the delicacies of this world. We can appreciate the good things this world offers, but our eyes are fixed on the other world—the world to come.

You can enjoy God's good gifts, but they don't have to be your god.

God created the world—that includes you. And God delights in His creation—that also includes you, whom He created in His own image.

That means you are different from anything else in all of His creation. You're not on equal footing with a beetle, a poodle, or a chimpanzee. You have the stamp of God on your very soul!

That also means you have an incredible dignity and value as God's image bearer. In fact, humans are the only created beings whom God invites to have a relationship with Him. God places people at the pinnacle of all creation—and He wants to spend time with *you.*

God welcomes you to partake in the perfect fellowship of the Trinity—a fellowship that has existed from eternity past and will never end.

Incredible.

Oh, and as a side benefit to all that, you also get to enjoy the blessings of His earthly creation.

See? I told you every great story has a beginning. And in the next chapter, we'll continue our journey as we take a look at another fundamental question of our existence: *Why are you here?*

QUESTION 2
Why Are You Here?

What's the most powerful movie you've seen in the last five years? Think about it. Perhaps it was an Oscar winner that everyone talked about. Or maybe your mind immediately went to a lesser-known film that spoke to you.

Do you have the movie in your mind? Okay, now ask yourself, *What was this movie's point? What goal did it achieve? Why was it so moving?*

Every film has a purpose. And all the elements of a movie—sound, lighting, music, acting, etc.—work together like an orchestra to produce the intended result. And it all happens under the authority of the director.

When you consider the story of your life and the role you play in this world, the question that naturally comes to mind is, "What purpose does the Director (God) have for me? What goal am I supposed to achieve?"

Why am I here?

Of all the soul-searching questions people ask about their lives, this one is the most common. That's because we all have a deep desire to understand the reason for our existence.

As I shared in the previous chapter, the reason we're here is deeply rooted in our origins. Remember the conversation the three persons of the Trinity had in Genesis 1:26…

> *"Let us make human beings in our image, to be like us. They will reign over the fish in the sea, the birds in the sky, the livestock, all the wild animals on the earth, and the small animals that scurry along the ground."* (NLT)

I could spend the rest of this book unpacking the idea of the Trinity and never even scratch the surface. It's an incredibly deep theological teaching that's been embraced from the earliest moments in church history: God is three persons in one.

I don't have the space to really unpack this truth here, so let me define it very quickly with this statement from the Athanasian Creed from early church history:

> *For there is one Person of the Father, another of the Son, and another of the Holy Ghost. But the Godhead of the Father, of the Son, and of the Holy*

Ghost, is all one; the Glory equal, the Majesty co-eternal.

As I touched on in the first chapter of this book, these three persons—Father, Son, and Holy Spirit—coexisted completely in themselves before creation. They were fully satisfied. This means we weren't created because God was lonely or bored. He already had all the fellowship He needed.

The Essence of Your Created Purpose

You might know that the Bible was written in three ancient languages—Hebrew, a little Aramaic, and Greek—and the book of Genesis was composed entirely in Hebrew.

But if you ask someone who knows a lot about ancient languages, they'll tell you that translating them into English can pose some challenges, particularly because one word in Hebrew might have more than one meaning in English.

This is partly why we have several Bible translations. The most popular modern English translation today is the New International Version (NIV). There's also the English Standard Version (ESV), a paraphrased translation called *The Message* (MSG), and the one I use most often is the New Living Translation (NLT).

It's really interesting to read Genesis 1:26 in

different translations. The NLT, which I used on page 24, says, "Let us make human beings in our image, to be like us."

The ESV puts it a different way: "Let us make man in our image, after our likeness." And *The Message*, which is more of a paraphrase, reads, "Let us make human beings in our image, make them reflecting our nature…."

As we read these three versions, we begin to capture the essence of the original Hebrew. Basically, God is saying, "I created people to be like us and to reflect our very nature. That was the original purpose."

You'll want to bookmark that in your mind because it provides the foundation for everything that follows in this book.

Let's move on to Genesis 1:28…

> *Then God blessed them and said, "Be fruitful and multiply. Fill the earth and govern it. Reign over the fish in the sea, the birds in the sky, and all the animals that scurry along the ground."* (NLT)

What do we see here? We see purpose, meaning, and the answer to one of the Four Big Cosmic Questions: "Why am I here? Am I here on accident—the result of cosmic chance? Or is it possible that the God who created me also has a dream and a purpose for me?"

Rick Warren, well-known pastor and author, published a book in 2002 called *The Purpose Driven Life*. This book gained immense popularity—so much so that a 2005 survey by George Barna found that pastors named it as the single most influential book on their lives and ministries.

So what made *The Purpose Driven Life* so popular? What was the hook that drew people in? Take a look at the book's subtitle: *What on Earth Am I Here For?*

More than 30 million copies of this book have been sold because it taps into a question our souls are itching to answer. It brings to life the struggle each of us faces: *Is there something more to this life?*

The Bible says yes.

Most people today are chasing after lesser purposes. But God has a big, big purpose for you—one that will make your life look completely different if you choose to fully embrace it.

Think of it this way: Let's say you and I are neighbors. You knock on my door one afternoon to ask if you can borrow a chainsaw, because you have a tree you need to cut down. So I say, "Of course," and bring it out to you.

You take a look at the chainsaw and ask, "Is it a good chainsaw? Will it get the job done?"

I say, "Absolutely. Look how shiny it is. It looks so nice sitting on the shelf in my garage. And the other day, I took it down and it sounded great when I started it up. In fact, I even used it to cut a loaf of bread."

You'd look at me like I'd lost my mind! Because what makes a great chainsaw isn't how good it looks, how nice it sounds when it starts up, or if it can cut a loaf of bread. A great chainsaw is one that cuts wood… and does it well!

Many—probably even most—people today are "nice chainsaws" just sitting on the shelf of life. So it's no wonder they experience so much discontentment. They're not cutting wood like they're designed to do. They were made to live one way, but they're living against the grain of their creation.

God speaks into that situation and says, "Go with the grain for which I created you. If you're a chainsaw, let's start cutting wood. If you're a bird-dog, let's hunt instead of chasing squirrels. Let's figure out what your purpose is so you can experience the joy and happiness that can fill your life when you live it out."

Are you beginning to see the picture?

Wrestling with the Competing Story

There's another story that begs for our attention and tries to draw us away from God's plans and dreams for our lives. It comes from the camp that says, "There is no God. When I die, it's over. So that's how I'm going to live. I place my faith in me."

Atheists like Stephen Hawking and Richard Dawkins would openly advocate this view. And in believing we're an accident, I'm convinced they rob themselves and their followers of real meaning in life.

The only purpose and meaning an atheist can have is one that's birthed entirely in his own ideas, opinions, or emotions. There is no soul, and there is no cosmic truth.

If this were true, then it would be possible to conclude that both Hitler and Gandhi must have fulfilled their purpose in life so long as they did what their minds told them to do. They followed their own ideas, emotions, and opinions. What a dangerous and destructive way of thinking!

There was a brilliant English philosopher by the name of Bertrand Russell. He died in 1970, but he was extremely honest about the logical conclusions of his atheistic beliefs. Because he didn't believe in God, he had no authoritative

faith in anything at all. And yet he understood the implications of his worldview. He openly argued, "Unless you assume a God, the question of life's purpose is meaningless." So even Bertrand Russell would have to admit that the only way to find real purpose in life is to believe in God.

How you think matters. That's because what you believe impacts the way you live your life. It shapes the way you parent, it informs your politics, and it guides your morality.

Fyodor Dostoevsky, the great Russian writer and outspoken Christian, said, "If God does not exist, then everything is permitted." It's impossible to have a true moral authority if there's no God. In fact, who are we to tell anyone what he or she can or can't do?

Furthermore, if there's no God, then what separates us from the animals? Wouldn't we just be a herd of humanity, walking and grazing on this rock we call Earth, spinning in the cosmos around a star that's eventually going to die?

I'd even go so far as to say that if we really are nothing but a species that has risen out of the chaotic cosmos by chance, then what would be wrong with making our species as superior as we can? Why not weed out the weak and the less desirable traits?

We're less than a century removed from

an ideology that tried to do just that—not in the jungles of Africa or the tribal regions of Afghanistan, but in Western Europe. The Nazi regime in Germany, though they proclaimed to be aligned with the Church (a claim made for political reasons), embraced the atheism of Charles Darwin and Friedrich Nietzsche. We look back today, and we're horrified by what happened. But let us never become so ignorant as to believe our society today isn't capable of even greater evils.

God, in staunch opposition to Darwin and Nietzsche, says, "You are made in My image—no matter where you come from or what you look like." And when we understand that God has stamped every single person with His divine image, we begin to see dignity in everyone.

How we think about God determines our purpose. And our purpose determines whether or not we treat others with dignity.

So our job, as followers of Jesus Christ, is to discover our God-given purpose and show others they have a God-given dignity. They may be scarred, broken, and shredded by sin, but they're never too far gone for God's grace.

So Why Were You Created?

We've established that we're created, and that means God has a purpose and a dream for our lives. So where can we begin to discover that purpose? A great place to start is 1 Corinthians 10:31…

> *So whether you eat or drink, or whatever you do, do it all for the glory of God.* (NLT)

If the apostle Paul were here today, we'd be able to ask him, "What do you mean by this?" And I'm pretty sure his answer would be, "I'm just talking about Genesis 1. I'm saying you were made to be satisfied and happy in God in everything you do."

It's interesting when we look at the word *glory*. It's one of those words we've heard before, but it's really hard to define. It wasn't on our third grade vocabulary list. So let's take a few minutes to explore *what* it is before we figure out *how* we do it!

If we look into the Old Testament, we see God's glory is a manifested presence of the person of God. Moses experienced God's glory firsthand on Mount Sinai. The Scripture tells us in Exodus 34:29-30…

> *When Moses came down Mount Sinai carrying the two stone tablets inscribed with the terms of the covenant, he wasn't*

> *aware that his face had become radiant because he had spoken to the LORD. So when Aaron and the people of Israel saw the radiance of Moses' face, they were afraid to come near him.* (NLT)

Moses experienced the manifested presence of the person of God—His glory. And when we glorify God, we become that sort of experience to someone else. In the way we act, feel, and think, we become a manifestation of God's character to the world. We show others who He is and what He's like.

Do you see the parallel to Genesis 1:26? God created us to "be like" Him. You are not God, but you are a reflection of His character and His nature. In everything you do, you are a signpost that points to Him. So when others interact with you, they walk away thinking, *Something is different about that person.*

We Have a "Glory Problem"

One of the greatest disconnects I see in the Church today is a significant number of people who've received God's blessings, yet refuse to use those blessings to point other people back to God. I call this the "glory problem."

Take, for example, the successful businessperson who makes a lot of money and gives generously. Yet when you talk with him or

her, all you hear is "I did this" and "I did that." There's no sense of a need to reflect God in his or her giftedness—and use it to point others to Jesus Christ. But we know those gifts that gave this person such success came directly from God.

Who do you think wired you this way? Who gave you your abilities and talents? Whether you're an artist, an accountant, a barista, or a doctor, you have the skills you have because God gave them to you.

That, my friend, is what we call "unmerited favor." The Bible calls it "grace"—and it's responsible for everything you do.

*You live, breathe, work, and sleep **by** God's grace and **for** His glory.*

The Westminster Catechism, written in the mid-1600s, puts it this way: "The chief end of man is to glorify God and enjoy him forever." That means when you glorify God, enjoying Him forever just happens. The more you utilize your God-given gifts and reflect Him in the process, the more happy and fulfilled you'll be in your life.

That's God's dream for you.

Your Place in God's Big Story

We're beginning to scratch the surface of what God's purpose and dream for your life really is. But before we go any further, it's important that you understand where you and I fit in the big story—what theologians call God's "metanarrative" of Scripture.

This big story—like any good theatrical work—has different acts, as well as scenes within those acts. So let me share what I believe are the six big acts we'll find as we make our way through the story of the Bible.

Act 1: Creation

This story, which we spent a lot of time on in the first chapter of this book, begins in Genesis 1. God created the world new and beautiful. There was no pain or suffering, and people lived in unhindered fellowship with God—as well as with each other. Unfortunately, this story only lasts two chapters in the Bible before things go terribly wrong.

Act 2: Devastation

Something went sideways in this wonderful existence—Adam and Eve disobeyed God and ate that forbidden fruit, and then evil and suffering entered the world. The act itself was a rebellion, a rejection, and an attempt to take

control of God's created order for themselves.

This period of devastation lasts nine chapters—and it's a complete bloodbath. There was terrible brutality, violence, and continued rebellion against God and His people. It got so bad that God sent a flood to wipe out the whole world—sparing only Noah and his family. But even after that, the problem of sin continued in the generations that followed. This is the opposite of what God intended.

If you're a little confused about Act 2, hang with me. I'll discuss it in greater depth in the next chapter!

Act 3: Reconciliation, Part 1

Then our story takes an interesting turn. Instead of bringing judgment on the world, God spoke to a man named Abram in Genesis 12:1-3 and told him…

> *"Leave your native country, your relatives, and your father's family, and go to the land that I will show you. I will make you into a great nation. I will bless you and make you famous, and you will be a blessing to others. I will bless those who bless you and curse those who treat you with contempt. All the families on earth will be blessed through you."* (NLT)

God told Abram, "I'm going to kick this off

with you. You are going to have a big family—and your family is going to be a blessing to the whole world. You'll show others what it's like to know Me."

Eventually, God gave Abram the name "Abraham," which means "father of many nations" (Genesis 17). And his descendants were known as the nation of Israel, to whom was given the responsibility of showing the world who God is.

This is one of the most pivotal moments in the entire Bible because as we work our way from this point forward in the Old Testament, we're introduced to great heroes from the line of Abraham—heroes like David.

You've probably heard the story of how David came on the scene, stepping up to fight the Philistine giant Goliath. He was the youngest and smallest of his brothers, but his faith in God compelled him to defend the people of Israel from the domineering Philistine army. So with a sling and a stone, he killed Goliath on the battlefield and saved Israel.

Yet like most of the heroes in Abraham's family, David had some deep struggles. He was utterly human, and he wrestled throughout his life with the curse of Genesis 3. In what was probably his darkest moment, he slept with another man's wife, got her pregnant, and then had the man sent to the front lines of battle so he'd be killed.

But David's failures, however heinous they were, didn't define him. He confessed his brokenness and sinfulness, sought God for forgiveness, and experienced God's mercy in a way few people ever have.

Many years later, we read about an Israelite boy named Daniel and his friends Shadrach, Meshach, and Abednego. These four young men lived during a terrible time for Israel, when the nation had been sacked by the Babylonians and was taken into exile. And though they were commanded to adopt the Babylonian way of life, they remained faithful to God—and were miraculously spared from execution.

The Old Testament is filled with story after story of faithful men and women—descendants of Abraham—who understood their blessing *and* their responsibility to be a blessing to the world. And throughout Act 3, we see a crescendo of promises of a coming Redeemer who would overcome sin and brokenness once and for all.

Act 4: Reconciliation, Part 2

In a tiny suburb of Jerusalem called Bethlehem, a child was born. It's here that the crescendo of the Old Testament reaches its climax. This baby, Jesus, was untouched by sin. He grew to manhood, healed the sick, restored sight to the blind, raised the dead, and demonstrated that He has control over all of creation.

He was the Son of God, the second person of the Trinity, who came to earth as a human being.

The apostle Paul would eventually call Him "the last Adam" (1 Corinthians 15:45 NLT) because Jesus shows us what it would be like if the first Adam had never rejected God. And with His death on the cross, Jesus paid the penalty for Adam's sin—and ours—once and for all. He took all of the devastation—past, present, and future—upon His shoulders on that cross.

Every sin you've ever committed was on His shoulders. And after three days, He rose from the dead to show the world that death has been defeated forever.

Act 5: Renewal

After the resurrection of Jesus, He told His followers (whom He called the "church") to go out and share His message of salvation with the world (Matthew 28:19-20). And in the days that followed, God sent the Holy Spirit, the third person of the Trinity, to live inside believers in Christ and empower them to carry out that work of taking the Gospel to all nations.

So the early church began to spread quickly… with believers all over modern-day Israel, Europe, Turkey, and very likely India within one generation after Jesus. People of many nations began to experience what it's like

to love Jesus, and they showed others how to follow Him.

Act 6: Restoration

The sixth act is where God's promises throughout the book of Revelation and many other places are finally realized—and all things are made new (Revelation 21:5). The prophet Isaiah, describing what this time will be like, writes in Isaiah 25:6-8…

> *In Jerusalem, the LORD of Heaven's Armies*
> *will spread a wonderful feast*
> *for all the people of the world.*
> *It will be a delicious banquet*
> *with clear, well-aged wine and choice meat.*
> *There he will remove the cloud of gloom,*
> *the shadow of death that hangs over the earth.*
> *He will swallow up death forever!*
> *The Sovereign LORD will wipe away all tears.*
> *He will remove forever all insults and mockery*
> *against his land and people.*
> *The LORD has spoken!* (NLT)

This isn't some Casper the Friendly Ghost view of eternity, where we'll be floating on clouds and playing our harps. This is a party that lasts forever. And in that forever, the curse of Adam will be gone. Satan will be destroyed. There will be no more pain and no more death. And while we will work, we'll never ever toil again!

So Where Are We in the Story?

Today, you and I are in the middle of the fifth act of this big Good News story. We exist between the cross and the second coming, and we are intricately written into this story because we have an expressed purpose: to reflect God to the world.

Let's make it a little more tangible. Theologian N. T. Wright uses the imaginary illustration of a Shakespearean play that was lost. The play had been rumored to exist, but over the years people debated whether it was ever written.

So one day, a scholar rummaging through some of Shakespeare's old manuscripts found the lost play. It was in Shakespeare's handwriting—so it's undoubtedly his. But there's one problem with this manuscript—it was missing Act 5.

What do you think we'd do? Would we roll up that manuscript, put it on the shelf, and refuse to perform it? Absolutely not! Even an incomplete manuscript from Shakespeare is incredibly valuable!

Here's what would happen: A Shakespearean acting company would take that manuscript and perform Act 1 just as it was written. Then they'd do the same with Acts 2, 3,

and 4. After that, they'd look at Act 6, see how the play turns out, and then fill in the blanks however they think it should go.

That's a lot like what we're doing today. We see the first four acts—their failures, successes, highs, and lows—and we seek to be faithful to what's been written with everything we do today.

But if we're going to do this well and stay true to the original intent, we have to be mindful. We're mindful of how the first acts were written, as well as the last one. And through those acts, we discover the intent of the Author, God. So we play our role in the story in a way that connects the first acts to the final one.

Now life here in Act 5 isn't easy. It's filled with hopelessness, pain, hardship, and sin. But there's hope for those who are believers in Christ—and that hope is that everything will be resolved in Act 6. This isn't the end!

Remember that when you're dealing with chronic pain. Remember it when someone close to you passes away. Remember it when you have what my wife Susan and I call a "broken world moment" that just plain hurts.

There's still another act to come!

Our lives may last 70, 80, or 90 years if God gives us that amount of time. And when it's over,

we'll look back from eternity and it will all seem like it was a blink. The suffering we experienced on earth will pale in comparison to the glory we'll experience in heaven.

Having that perspective changes how you live your life. It rearranges your priorities and puts your hardships in context. And as you spend time reading the Bible, you start to see every experience you have as a signpost to eternity with God.

Even in your failures, like King David, you can understand that your shortcomings don't define you. That's because your greatest earthly accomplishment won't be your success, but maintaining the heart of God throughout your failures and successes. So you remain humbly mindful that even when you're on top of the world, temptations aren't far off!

Friend, that is what it means to glorify God. It means you're in His story and are privileged to be able to pen a paragraph in His drama. It means that God invites us in from the very beginning and gives us a place on the stage of His story.

What song will you sing? What lines will you deliver? You're free to contribute however you feel led—that's the freedom you have in Jesus Christ.

When you connect God's story to yours, you begin to live with true freedom.

What It Means to Live Truly Free

I love the illustration that pastor and author Tim Keller gives about freedom. If you ever watch eagles flying through the air… seeing them hit those thermals that shoot them up into the sky… it's incredible. An eagle flies unhindered, unencumbered, gracefully, and beautifully. It's no wonder America's Founding Fathers chose the eagle as the symbol of our freedom.

As followers of Christ, we fly in the thermals of life. The Bible says we're seated "in the heavenly realms because we are united with Christ Jesus" (Ephesians 2:6 NLT).

Unfortunately, I know a lot of people who've been soaring like eagles with their wings spread out, being shot up into the air by those thermals. But then they look down and think, *Those chickens on the ground sure look like they're having fun.*

Over time, that thought takes root in their mind. So they begin to wonder if the thermals they're hitting are really all that great. Then they make the decision to descend to earth and start walking in their own way—the ways of the world.

That's a life sustained on our own efforts. It's a life that doesn't believe God has the best plan for us. And let me tell you, it's no life at all. You're expending effort that God doesn't want

you to expend. Not only that, but you're also making yourself vulnerable to predators (like Satan and his demons) who will take you out the first chance they get!

In Christ, you cease to be a chicken and instead become a majestic eagle. Even the Bible tells us in Isaiah 40:31…

> *But those who trust in the LORD will find new strength.*
> *They will soar high on wings like eagles.*
> *They will run and not grow weary.*
> *They will walk and not faint.* (NLT)

Choose daily to trust God to fulfill you in every way. Submit your plans, your desires, and your entire life to Him and say, "God, may everything I do be for Your glory."

Do that, and you'll soar!

Now, I know you might be thinking, *Brandon, that sounds amazing. But if God created everything perfectly and I'm meant to enjoy creation, then why is there pain and suffering in the world?* ***How did it all go wrong?***

We'll answer that Big Cosmic Question in the next chapter.

QUESTION 3
How Did It All Go Wrong?

You may remember when the news broke about the earthquake in Port-au-Prince, Haiti, in 2010. That earthquake killed over 300,000 people. I had the opportunity to be part of a relief trip to Haiti in the months after the quake, and what I saw was devastating.

The most heartbreaking part had to be the orphans. I saw so many small children walking alone, crying and looking for their parents, desperate for help.

Then we look at our own bodies and see disease. Smallpox killed more than 300 million through the generations. Spanish Flu killed 50 million. And how many of us have been—or know someone who's been—impacted by diseases like cancer and HIV?

Yes, something *is* wrong. Something is broken in our world. So how do we explain it?

Well, we learned from Genesis 1 that you and I are made in God's image and have access to all the benefits and blessings that come with that.

We were created like mirrors to reflect God to the world. But we have a problem: something has gone wrong with that mirror. And as a result, the world that image is reflected into isn't as it should be.

What World Religions Say About Evil

Different religions have put forward a number of ideas to explain the problem of evil and suffering.

Hinduism says, "Suffering now is the result of evil in your past, and you're on the cosmic karma wheel of reaping what you've sown. So your job is just to endure your suffering in this life, and maybe you'll have a better life when you're reincarnated."

Buddha got sick and tired of this cosmic karma wheel. So he began teaching a different philosophy: This whole world is really an illusion, and if you'll focus enough, you'll reach an enlightened state and be able to transcend this physical world.

Then there's Taoism—which is where we get that yin and yang so many people have tattooed on their backs. Taoism says suffering is just the other side of pleasure. So if you've had a great day, then a really bad day is on its way. And at the end of your life, your good days and bad days will all be balanced out.

Now, of course there are many more religions and philosophies that deal with the subject of suffering and evil. But I want to take some time to share what the Bible says about these issues, and why I believe it's by far the best explanation of the problem of pain in the world today.

The Real Root of the Problem

You remember the story from Genesis 1 and 2—that God created the world perfectly and created people to inhabit this perfect world in unhindered fellowship with Him. When we come to Genesis 3, we see a tragic turn in the story—the place where it all went wrong. Take a look at verse 1…

> *The serpent was the shrewdest of all the wild animals the LORD God had made. One day he asked the woman, "Did God really say you must not eat the fruit from any of the trees in the garden?"* (NLT)

This is poetic language describing Satan, our enemy, the devil. It's the first time he appears in Scripture, and he's already lying. God never said that Adam and Eve couldn't eat from any of the trees—just one tree (Genesis 2:16-17).

We don't know how many trees were in the garden with Adam and Eve (it could have been billions), but God gave them every one of

them—except for one.

Here, Satan is trying to turn Eve against God by portraying Him as harsh and unloving, when in fact God was unbelievably generous. The enemy twists that generosity to make it look like selfishness.

But Eve tries to set the record straight in Genesis 3:2-3…

> *"Of course we may eat fruit from the trees in the garden," the woman replied. "It's only the fruit from the tree in the middle of the garden that we are not allowed to eat. God said, 'You must not eat it or even touch it; if you do, you will die.'"* (NLT)

Then Satan fires back in verses 4-5…

> *"You won't die!" the serpent replied to the woman. "God knows that your eyes will be opened as soon as you eat it, and you will be like God, knowing both good and evil."* (NLT)

He lies again. And this time, Eve believes it. Look at verse 6…

> *The woman was convinced. She saw that the tree was beautiful and its fruit looked delicious, and she wanted the wisdom it*

would give her. So she took some of the fruit and ate it. Then she gave some to her husband, who was with her, and he ate it, too. (NLT)

She looked at it, saw it was delicious, and took a bite. Then she gave some to her husband who, we're told, "was with her."

Pause right there for a moment.

It's wasn't just Eve who fell into sin. Adam was right there with her. And he could have stepped in at any moment and said, "Honey, I know you're new here, but we're not going to eat that fruit."

But Adam didn't step in. Instead, he stayed silent. And when Eve ate, Adam ate too.

Everything Falls Apart

As a result of Adam and Eve's disobedience, things begin falling apart. Look at verse 7…

At that moment their eyes were opened, and they suddenly felt shame at their nakedness. So they sewed fig leaves together to cover themselves. (NLT)

Notice the first broken emotion Adam and Eve felt in their fallen state: *shame*. It was the first of many. And when God came back on the

scene, things really took a turn. Take a look at verses 8-9…

> *When the cool evening breezes were blowing, the man and his wife heard the LORD God walking about in the garden. So they hid from the LORD God among the trees. Then the LORD God called to the man, "Where are you?"* (NLT)

Now, God already knew where Adam and Eve had gone. He could smell the stench of sin in the air. He recognized that His order had been violated—that creation itself was crumbling.

So why did He ask, *"Where are you?"*

It was out of His kindness.

Like a parent lovingly draws the truth from the child instead of harshly scolding him when he's done wrong, God draws the truth out of Adam and Eve so they'll understand the gravity of what they've done. He could've rolled in with thunder, lightning, and judgment—but He chose not to.

With that picture of God in mind, let's continue reading Genesis 3:10-13…

> *[Adam] replied, "I heard you walking in the garden, so I hid. I was afraid because I was naked."*

"Who told you that you were naked?" the LORD God asked. "Have you eaten from the tree whose fruit I commanded you not to eat?"

The man replied, "It was the woman you gave me who gave me the fruit, and I ate it."

Then the LORD God asked the woman, "What have you done?"

"The serpent deceived me," she replied. "That's why I ate it."

First, Adam and Eve felt shame, and here they began to blame—just like a child. Instead of owning up to their mistakes, both the man and the woman portrayed themselves as the victim.

Doesn't that sound like an argument you've been in? Of course, we've all been there. Whether with our kids, our spouse, a coworker, or a friend, we've all heard the "It's not my fault" excuse.

And if we're honest, we've all used it as well!

Throughout the rest of Genesis chapter 3, we see the impact that sin begins to have on the world. First, God pronounces curses on the serpent, on the woman, and then on the man. He explains to the woman that she will experience

pain in bearing children (verse 16). And He tells the man that his work will no longer be pleasurable all the time, but he will struggle (verses 17-19).

So the curse of sin begins to take root in the world.

God's Grace Shows Up

In the midst of all these curses, it's critical that we remember what God said His punishment for sin would be. He clearly stated that if they ate from the fruit of the forbidden tree, they were "sure to die" (Genesis 2:17 NLT).

That's important because it means everything God does in chapter 3 is an act of grace. He could have ended Adam and Eve—along with the entire human race—right then and there.

But instead, He showed them grace by allowing them to live.

And in His grace, God put together a plan for the man and woman to continue living. He begins to roll it out in Genesis 3:20-21…

> *Then the man—Adam—named his wife Eve, because she would be the mother of all who live. And the LORD God made clothing from animal skins for Adam and his wife.*

It's important to note here that our attempts to cover our own shame will always be inadequate. God is the only One who can truly cover our shame. And how did He cover Adam and Eve's sin and shame? He shed the blood of an animal.

What an incredible picture of the need for a sacrifice!

Of course, this points us to Jesus whose blood would also be shed to cover our sin and shame. Even here in the garden, we can see the beginnings of God's big rescue plan.

So God sent Adam and Eve out of the garden—again, in His mercy—because He didn't want them to live forever in their sin.

Why Would God Allow Evil?

One question I hear every time I preach on this is, "Brandon, why would a big, all-powerful, all-loving God allow things to go so wrong?" And sadly, this question causes a lot of people to conclude there can't be a God or that He can't be trusted.

So how do we answer the question of evil?

First, it's important to admit that our capacity to understand and explain evil and suffering in the world is irrelevant to whether

or not God exists. And just because we haven't heard an explanation that makes us happy, that doesn't mean there isn't one.

My kids come to me all the time asking for an explanation for why I did this or that. And there are some questions they ask that only life experience can answer. So I've come up with a way of explaining it to them. I tell them, "That answer is too big for your suitcase right now. You can't pack it in." It's very possible we don't fully understand evil because we don't have the capacity to do so at this point.

Another answer to the question of evil is that the presence of evil doesn't point away from God—it actually points to Him.

There's a philosopher at the University of Notre Dame named Alvin Plantinga who puts this idea forward. His reasoning is that if you don't have God determining what's good and what's evil, then you can't call *anything* good or evil.

Therefore, the fact that we *can* call something "good" or "evil" is evidence of a moral God.

Take, for example, a man who decides he's going to have an affair. He feels like his wife is a different person than the woman he fell in love with years ago. He hates his marriage, he knows in his heart that he deserves to be happy—and

another woman at work makes him feel that way. So he cheats on his wife. And in his mind, he's morally justified in doing so.

Just about anyone would objectively say that's not right. But without a universal moral standard, who is anyone to say what's good and what's evil? Someone may say, "But he broke his wedding vows, which is wrong." But we can't even say *that* is wrong unless there is objective moral truth.

Therefore, in order to say something is evil, we must claim there's a moral absolute—and ultimately, that absolute must be God.

C. S. Lewis advanced this idea in his book *Mere Christianity*. He claims that within each of us, there is a moral "ought"—a code. And if there's a moral code, then there's a writer of that code. So we can know what's right and wrong because God has written it on our hearts.

So How Do We Deal with Evil and Suffering?

All of this theological talk is great. But let's bring it down to the nuts and bolts. How do we, as people living in this fallen and broken world, deal personally with the problems of evil and suffering?

When suffering knocks at your door—

maybe someone you care about is sick, a friend betrayed you, or you lost someone you love—how do you respond?

You can take comfort in the words of 1 Peter 1:6-7…

> *So be truly glad. There is wonderful joy ahead, even though you must endure many trials for a little while. These trials will show that your faith is genuine. It is being tested as fire tests and purifies gold—though your faith is far more precious than mere gold. So when your faith remains strong through many trials, it will bring you much praise and glory and honor on the day when Jesus Christ is revealed to the whole world.* (NLT)

I talked at the beginning of this chapter about what my wife and I call a "broken world moment." It's what we say to each other when we experience evil or suffering: "This is a broken world moment." We do it to remind ourselves of the big story at hand—that God made the world and everything in it good, our sin caused it to break, and God has a plan to heal it all.

And if you'll embrace His story for your life, then you can also go there whenever you're struggling. You can remember, *I'm in a story that began way before me. And this struggle with evil and suffering is a part of that story.*

I've had the opportunity to meet with many engaged couples over the years. And I can't tell you how many times I've heard a young man or woman say, "I could never forgive something like infidelity. If that ever happens, I'm out."

I caution people who say that, because God has the power to give you love and grace that will endure the worst moments you can imagine. And that doesn't just apply to marital infidelity. Whatever "broken world moment" you face, God can give you supernatural grace and love to get through it.

When those moments hit, rest in God's promises. Write them on your mirror. Put them on your phone. Stick them on your fridge. Because God's promises never fail! And He's promised in Jeremiah 29:11…

> *"For I know the plans I have for you," says the LORD. "They are plans for good and not for disaster, to give you a future and a hope."* (NLT)

The greatest exercise you can do when you're suffering is to go to the cross of Christ. Remember the covering He provides for your shame. Take heart in the love and compassion He showed you by dying in your place.

The God of the Bible doesn't say, "Work your

way back to Me," when you've been broken. *No, He has already worked His way to you!*

I was emailing recently with a close friend who struggles with "broken world moments" every day in the form of constant physical pain. He'll most likely deal with it for the rest of his life—unless of course the Lord heals him. And he takes comfort in the fact that even if God doesn't heal him on this earth, he has a pain-free eternity to look forward to with Jesus Christ.

One day, we'll look back on this life and realize it was only a blink in the scope of eternity. That's exactly what the apostle Paul was talking about when he wrote, "Yet what we suffer now is nothing compared to the glory he will reveal to us later" (Romans 8:18).

Christianity is not a problem-free faith. It is a faith that says God will walk with you through your problems.

It's a faith that says God is with you in the storms.

God Is Not Done with Us Yet

The moment Adam and Eve fell, God looked into their eyes and He saw us. And although every generation rightly prays, "God, come back soon," the truth is that He's not done yet. He still has more people to save!

So until the day when He returns, we have to remain anchored in Him. The storms of life are going to hit. And when they do, you'll either be tossed and turned by the circumstances of life, or you'll cling faithfully to the solid Rock, Jesus Christ. The choice is yours.

That's why 2 Corinthians 4:8-10 says…

We are pressed on every side by troubles, but we are not crushed. We are perplexed, but not driven to despair. We are hunted down, but never abandoned by God. We get knocked down, but we are not destroyed. Through suffering, our bodies continue to share in the death of Jesus so that the life of Jesus may also be seen in our bodies. (NLT)

Friend, that is our anchor… *the life of Jesus seen in our bodies*.

Charles Spurgeon, the great 19th century preacher from London, put it this way: "God is too good to be unkind and He is too wise to be mistaken. And when we cannot trace His hand, we must trust His heart."

In our moments of deepest despair, God's grace goes deeper still.

Now let's get ready to complete our journey by exploring the final Big Cosmic Question: *Where are you going?*

QUESTION 4
Where Are You Going?

Church history is filled with stories of faithful men and women who did incredible things for the Gospel. I particularly find one early church leader named Polycarp utterly fascinating.

Mentored by the apostle John, Polycarp lived a long life and had an incredible ministry. According to *The Martyrdom of Polycarp*, he was asked to deny Jesus under the threat of death. And tradition tells us he replied, "Eighty-six years I have served him, and he has done me no wrong. How can I blaspheme my King and my Savior?" Then he was burned and stabbed to death.

How could Polycarp face his demise when a few simple words could have secured his freedom? Because he believed beyond the moment. He possessed a keen sense of what was beyond this life and the powerful weapon of Christian hope.

He knew where he was going.

The final soul-searching question is a big one. Even if we know where we came from

and understand why we're here, the question of where we're going is so pressing—because it's inescapable.

And because so many people can't answer it, they're absolutely terrified.

You see, we all will experience some sort of tragedy in our lives. And it's in those moments that people ponder what's ahead after we die. Some phrase it, "Is this all there is?"

Of course, the scientists and the super rich are throwing everything they have at this question.

I mentioned the famous scientist Stephen Hawking earlier in this book. He's proposed a formula for immortality: a transferral of consciousness. He believes we'll one day be able to take all of our thoughts and experiences and put them on a hard drive. Then, we'll exist forever as computers.

Then there are Google co-founders Sergey Brin and Larry Page who have founded a company called Calico. Calico is a biotech company created to stop aging dead in its tracks—and it has drawn investments in the hundreds of millions of dollars.

So the answer to immortality from science is to provide eternal life through technology. And the super rich believe the answer is to throw

money at the problem. Both of these groups are trying to answer the question, "How does this story end?"

I love going to museums. When I visit New York, one of my favorite things to do is get lost in the many museums there. And when you go to those museums, it becomes clear that different civilizations throughout history have struggled to answer that same question.

Well, God has an answer. In fact, I believe the biblical answer to the question of our future is the most complete of them all.

But to understand it, we have to go back to the beginning one more time.

Our Future Is Determined by Our Past

We began our story with a loving God who created all things and made them good. He made people with free will—the ability to choose. He didn't want you to be a robot.

But you can't have a choice without options. People couldn't truly choose to love God without the ability to choose *not* to love Him. So God essentially told them, "I'm going to give you the choice to go your own way, because real love is not a mandate."

Well, you know the story by now. Adam and

Eve chose to disobey, and they ate the forbidden fruit. That's where it all went wrong, and it sent a shockwave of sin throughout all of God's good created order of things.

God could have ended it right there, but He didn't. He promised a redeemer (the "offspring" of the woman in Genesis 3:15) who would come and heal the brokenness that mankind had brought about. Jesus came into the world to heal the sin in the hearts of man.

The Curse of Your Sin Is Removed

It's important to note again that no other world religion has anything close to what Christianity offers. Every other religion says, "Here's how you work your way to God. Here are the steps you take to make yourself acceptable to Him."

But the Bible teaches, "Here's how God worked His way to us. Here's how God showered us with life."

Christianity is completely different!

When Jesus died on the cross, He literally took your death upon His own shoulders. He tasted the wrath and the punishment of all sin on the cross. Then He came back to life to show the world that death has forever been defeated!

Jesus' resurrection was the real thing. His disciples touched Him. They ate with Him. And His resurrection body shows us what God is going to do one day—take all the physical and spiritual brokenness in the world, and make it new again. All the wrong things will be made right!

So in order for us to begin to understand where we're going, we have to first have that promise in mind—*God is going to make everything right*.

And everything being made right means death is gone. So what happens when we close our eyes in this world?

Well, if we've trusted Christ and had Jesus' cleansing blood applied to us, we awaken to something much, much greater.

What Happens When We Die?

So what is heaven like? We know it's eternity with God. But that begs the question, "What will that eternity be like? What will we do forever?"

The most vivid representation of heaven we see in Scripture is found in the book of Revelation. And as we read, a few things become clear. First, we won't be just floating on a cloud and playing a harp. In Revelation, we see people having conversations with God

and singing in heaven. It will be a vibrant place where every need we have will find its fulfillment.

Heaven is real—and if you are a follower of Christ, you'll get to experience it. One day, you'll wake up in God's presence and live forever with Him.

And the Bible teaches that in the fullness of time—when everyone God determines to be born has been born—He will bring heaven to earth and make all things new.

This biblical truth is too often ignored, but it's absolute. God's plan is not that we endure cancer and bombs and tsunamis and earthquakes forever. There's a plan to make it all new again.

God's Plan to Make All Things New

Scripture tells us in Revelation 21:1…

> *Then I saw a new heaven and a new earth, for the old heaven and the old earth had disappeared. And the sea was also gone.* (NLT)

I've always wondered about that last sentence. Does that mean there's no more water? Well, other places in Revelation refer to rivers and streams in heaven. So what's going on here?

We have to remember that in the first century (when Revelation was written), the sea was a scary place. Many believed that giant monsters inhabited their depths—a thought fueled by the times when people would leave on a boat and never come back.

So when we read there's no sea in heaven, it means all fear is gone. There's no more uncertainty and no more chaos.

Then we read in Revelation 21:2…

> *And I saw the holy city, the new Jerusalem, coming down from God out of heaven like a bride beautifully dressed for her husband.* (NLT)

Here we see God bringing heaven down to earth. He's not destroying the physical world, as some religions teach—He's restoring it!

This is miles away from a kind of dualistic thinking that spirit is good and matter is bad. The fact that God is making the world new again—restoring its former glory to how He originally intended it—shows He cares for the world.

Then there are verses 3-6 of Revelation 21…

I heard a loud shout from the throne, saying, "Look, God's home is now among

his people! He will live with them, and they will be his people. God himself will be with them. He will wipe every tear from their eyes, and there will be no more death or sorrow or crying or pain. All these things are gone forever." And the one sitting on the throne said, "Look, I am making everything new!" And then he said to me, "Write this down, for what I tell you is trustworthy and true." And he also said, "It is finished! I am the Alpha and the Omega—the Beginning and the End. To all who are thirsty I will give freely from the springs of the water of life." (NLT)

And verses 24-26 of Revelation 21 are especially interesting…

The nations will walk in its light, and the kings of the world will enter the city in all their glory. Its gates will never be closed at the end of day because there is no night there. And all the nations will bring their glory and honor into the city. (NLT)

The reason that passage is so interesting to me is because it's saying the kings of all the nations will bring the best part of their nations into the Holy City. In other words, you don't have to view this current reality as something that's eventually going to be thrown away. What you do today matters for eternity!

That's right, the things that you do well now will be preserved, protected, and will actually glorify God. The reason you're an accountant is to make sure all the numbers line up—because it brings glory to God.

The reason you're a landscaper is to make all the lines straight and pick all the weeds—because it brings glory to God.

The reason you're an architect is to build beautiful things that point people to the beauty of our Creator. That's kind of fun to think about, isn't it?

There's also a good part of me that wonders if some of the art and music we know today will be in the heavenly city. This passage makes it sound quite possible!

This is certainly a far cry from the image we have in our minds of a boring eternity.

Years ago, a particular *The Far Side* comic pictured people waiting in line to get into heaven, and one person turns to the other and says, "Are there any magazines?"

No, heaven won't need magazines!

So what's the point of knowing all this? Why does our future matter? The answer is summed up in one word: *Hope*. Hope empowers

you to make it through those difficult times. And it gives your life meaning and purpose.

The hope you have about tomorrow *greatly* impacts your life today.

The Power of Hope in Your Life Now

Tim Keller gives this illustration: Imagine you are brought into a room and told to sit down. Someone says, "I want you to sit on this assembly line and screw this widget into that wadget every day for ten hours a day. And at the end of a whole year of doing this, I'll pay you $20,000."

Then someone else walks into the room, and you hear that same person telling the new guy, "I want you to do the same thing—screw this widget into that wadget every day for ten hours a day. And at the end of a year, I'm going to pay you $20 million."

How long do you think you'd last doing that kind of monotonous work for a mere $20,000? But do you think you could do it for $20 million? I bet just about anyone would say yes to that!

Why is that? The behavior is the same. You're experiencing the same tedious monotony whether you get $20,000 or $20 million. The only difference is what's coming after.

You see, what you think is coming next really does impact you today.

Of course, that's a made-up illustration. But here's a real-life example from one of the tragic chapters in our nation's history.

Back during the years of slavery in America, slaves would often sing spiritual songs that had been passed down through the generations. These songs would rise up and provide the motivation to continue working long, hot, and punishing hours. And after a hard day of work, they'd often sing and dance more at night.

Frederick Douglass, a former slave himself, heard people commenting about how happy the slaves seemed. He wrote…

> *The remark in the olden time was not unfrequently made, that slaves were the most contented and happy laborers in the world, and their dancing and singing were referred to in proof of this alleged fact; but it was a great mistake to suppose them happy because they sometimes made those joyful noises.*

What he's saying is, if you were to walk up to the slaves and watch them working, you might assume they were happy with what they were being forced to do. But you'd be missing it entirely.

The African spirituals weren't sung from a place of contentment or happiness with one's circumstances. They came from somewhere else—a deep longing that only eternity could fulfill. Take the chorus of the most famous of these spiritual songs…

Swing low, sweet chariot,
Comin' for to carry me home;
Swing low, sweet chariot,
Comin' for to carry me home.

In other words, as I toil and as I work, swing low, sweet chariot! Come carry me home. Swing low in the midst of my labor and carry me home. Swing low in the midst of this injustice and carry me home. Swing low because I was torn away from my home. Come carry me home.

What they believed impacted everything about their lives—no matter how challenging and brutal their circumstances.

And as Christ-followers, these slaves had this authentic faith. They believed beyond the here and now—which gave them something that couldn't be explained. As you study the words of those spirituals, you'll see a lot of singing about the afterlife. Why? Because it gave them hope!

But let's take a further look back at the history of Christianity. Rodney Stark says in his book, *The Rise of Christianity*, that in AD

165, Christians made up around 6 percent of the Roman Empire. In that same year, a plague began that killed many people, and just a few decades later, another great plague hit.

One historian named Galen wrote that if you stayed with your loved one while they were sick in those days, you were signing your own death warrant. So once someone in a home got sick, the rest of the family would hit the road and leave the sick person to die alone.

As the crowds of people walked away from the sick, Galen writes, "There was a group of people who stayed. The Christians. While everybody else was walking out of the city, they stayed. They cared for our loved ones. And they dressed their wounds."

Then he writes, "And it was reasonable for them to stay because of their view of what came next."

Because of their view of eternity, the early Christians were willing to suffer in the here and now. And what happened? Through those two plagues, the number of Christians went from 6 percent of the population to 50 percent!

Why? Because their hope kept them in the room. They dressed wounds. They gave the sick water and food. When everyone else left, it was the followers of Jesus who stayed behind.

Hope told them to face unreasonable situations because there's a room beyond this room—that when they closed their eyes to this world, they would open their eyes in the presence of God.

Remember the words of 2 Corinthians 4:8-10 and 17…

> *We are pressed on every side by troubles, but we are not crushed. We are perplexed, but not driven to despair. We are hunted down, but never abandoned by God. We get knocked down, but we are not destroyed. Through suffering, our bodies continue to share in the death of Jesus so that the life of Jesus may also be seen in our bodies.... For our present troubles are small and won't last very long. Yet they produce for us a glory that vastly outweighs them and will last forever!* (NLT)

So how could those early Christians stay in the room when it could've meant certain death? How could those brothers and sisters in Christ who experienced slavery still sing those spirituals?

Hope.

And how can those Christians in the Middle East today… who are being hunted down and

put to death… not recant their confession of Christ before they perish? Because they believe in a moment beyond this moment, in a reality that's bigger than this reality.

Hope helps you. Hope powers you through the pain of life. Isaiah 65:17-19 is such an encouragement about what the days to come will bring…

> *"Look! I am creating new heavens and a new earth,*
> *and no one will even think about the old ones anymore.*
> *Be glad; rejoice forever in my creation!*
> *And look! I will create Jerusalem as a place of happiness.*
> *Her people will be a source of joy.*
> *I will rejoice over Jerusalem*
> *and delight in my people.*
> *And the sound of weeping and crying*
> *will be heard in it no more."* (NLT)

Today is a shadow of what's to come. And if we believe that, then you and I are only shadows of our future selves. There's a much more real you than you're experiencing today. The future you will be so much better than the current you!

I realize that's heavy stuff. But picture the eternal you looking back on your days here in this fallen world and thinking, *Wow, that person was so broken.* Just like how you sometimes

think today about how naïve and inexperienced your younger self was, you'll see yourself today in a much different light.

And in eternity, there will be no more wondering. You won't have to wonder if the economy is going to tank. You won't have to wonder who's going to be the next president. You won't have to wonder if your back pain will ever go away. Those days will be gone.

Can you imagine if the eternal you could talk with the current you today? Maybe the eternal you would say, "I've got a word for you… eternity is a total blast! Everything you're worried about today is really nothing at all. And all of those little pains you experience on a daily basis—they're gone forever. Just you wait!"

What a day it will be when Isaiah 25:6-8 becomes a reality…

> *In Jerusalem, the LORD of Heaven's Armies*
> *will spread a wonderful feast*
> *for all the people of the world.*
> *It will be a delicious banquet*
> *with clear, well-aged wine and choice meat.*
> *There he will remove the cloud of gloom,*
> *the shadow of death that hangs over*
> *the earth.*
> *He will swallow up death forever!*

The Sovereign LORD will wipe away
all tears.
He will remove forever all insults
and mockery
against his land and people.
The LORD has spoken!

Years ago, John Lennon wrote a song called "Imagine." And in it, Lennon sang…

Imagine there's no heaven.
It's easy if you try.
No hell below us.
Above us only sky.
Imagine all the people
Living for today…

It's a classic but deeply sad song. And in this life, we have a choice to either live according to "Imagine" or "Swing Low, Sweet Chariot." Let me share the rest of those lyrics with you…

Well, now I looked over Jordan and
what did I see
Comin' for to carry me home
There was a band of angels a comin'
after me
Comin' for to carry me home

Well, I'm sometimes up and I'm
sometimes down
Comin' for to carry me home
But I know my soul is heavenly bound
Comin' for to carry me home

Well, now if you get there before I do
Comin' for to carry me home
Tell all of my friends that I'm a
comin' too
Comin' for to carry me home

Swing low, sweet chariot
Comin' for to carry me home
Swing low, sweet chariot
Comin' for to carry me home
Well, now they're comin' for to carry
me home

Swing low. Make it right, God. I believe justice is coming. To every promise, there is a fulfillment. Swing low right where I am—because, Lord, I'm low.

Which song will you sing? Which music does your soul dance to? God gave you the power to choose your story. And I believe there's only one true story that endures: His story.

But only you can choose.

NOW WHAT?

As you've taken this journey with me through the pages of this book, my guess is you've had one of three reactions.

Maybe you're a believer in Jesus Christ, and learning more about your part in God's big story has been an encouragement to your faith. If so, that's awesome!

Perhaps you're a skeptic—even an atheist—and you don't really know what to do with what you've just read. If that's you, let me encourage you to continue investigating what God says about you. Read more about Jesus and what He teaches about sin, grace, and His plan for your life. I've found my answer there—and I truly believe you can too.

Or you may be that person who says, "I was a skeptic, but now I'm all in. These are the answers my soul was searching for. I'm ready to follow Jesus and make God's story my story—whatever struggles that may bring."

If that's you, the Bible says, "Everyone who calls on the name of the LORD will be saved"

(Romans 10:13 NLT). And if you truly believe in your heart that Jesus took away your sins on the cross, then you can have every assurance that you'll experience eternity with Him.

So make TODAY the most important day in your life's SOUL SEARCH. Right now, allow me to guide you in a conversation with God, a prayer that will unlock your God-given potential. In this moment you can trust God completely to deal with your brokenness and set you on a path that unlocks eternity in your heart!

Pray with me…

God, I know I am a sinner. I believe Jesus died for all of my sins. I may not have it all figured out, but I fully trust that Jesus conquered death and came back to life. Paying fully for my sin, You have resurrected me to a brand-new life. I embrace You as the Lord of my life. Adopt me now as Your son or daughter, and may I never be the same again!

For us all, may the same power that raised Jesus to new life, fill our lives to accomplish much more than we could ever imagine!

About the Author

Brandon Thomas is a visionary leader who's known for his ability to take complex biblical issues and present them with unique insight. He shares the life-changing message of God's Word in creative, practical ways with both humor and relevance.

Brandon earned his doctorate in church growth in 2004. Since then, he and his wife Susan, who is a licensed professional counselor specializing in marriage and women's counseling, founded Keystone Church and Passionate Life Ministries.

Brandon and Susan have three daughters and a son, and they treasure family time together.

Please let us know if you'd like more information about additional resources from Passionate Life Ministries! Contact us at:

Passionate Life Ministries
8237 Mid Cities Blvd.
North Richland Hills, TX 76182

passionatelife.com